W9-CFV-448

One if by Land

A Massachusetts Number Book

Written by Heidi E.Y. Stemple and Illustrated by Jeannie Brett

Sleeping Bear Press™
310 North Main Street, Suite 300
Chelsea, MI 48118
www.sleepingbearpress.com

THOMSON
GALE™

Printed and bound in China.

First Edition

10 9 8 7 6 5 4 3 2 1

Library of Congress Cataloging-in-Publication Data

Stemple, Heidi E. Y.
One if by land : a Massachusetts number book / written by Heidi E.Y. Stemple; illustrated by Jeannie Brett.
p. cm.
Summary: "Massachusetts state history, famous people, landmarks, and industry are introduced through poetry and numbers. Detailed expository text on each topic is also included"—Provided by publisher.
ISBN 1-58536-186-0
1. Massachusetts—Juvenile literature. 2. Counting—Juvenile literature. I. Brett, Jeannie. II. Title.

F64.3.S74 2006
974.4—dc22 2006002197

This book is for my mother. All my books are for my mother.
Because without her none of this would have been possible.
Thank you, I love you.

HEIDI

For my sisters Jan and Sophie and my sister-in-law Durbara.

JEANNIE

In 1620 the *Mayflower* carrying 102 Pilgrims made landfall on the shores of the New World in what is now Massachusetts. Legend has it that the Pilgrims' first steps were onto Plymouth Rock. Though in truth, they had first landed on Cape Cod and later moved north to Plymouth. Still, the legend has been passed down through generations of Americans.

In 1774 the rock that is the center of this story was going to be pulled by oxen to the Town Square for display. When it split in two, only the top was brought. En route to a new location, this time the Pilgrim Hall Museum in 1834, the top section fell and cracked. Pieces were sold and stolen as souvenirs before the two halves were reunited in 1880. Finally in 1921 they moved together to Pilgrim Memorial State Park where they sit today as a reminder of the Pilgrims' historic journey.

one 1

1 rock sits
on historic Plymouth Bay,
where the *Mayflower* landed
on the Pilgrims' first Day.

Black bears share a lot of territory with Massachusetts citizens, especially in the western part of the state. They have a keen sense of smell which helps them find food—sometimes in garbage cans and bird feeders. Once they find a spot with food, even if it's in someone's backyard, bears have an excellent memory and will likely return for seconds.

An adult male black bear can weigh as much as 600 pounds. The smaller female, called a sow, usually has two cubs and can be very protective of them. When she has the cubs with her, a mother black bear's natural instinct is to charge aggressively at whatever she considers a threat, but very seldom will a black bear actually attack. If you see a bear, you should never feed it because this is dangerous both for you *and* the bear.

2

2 black bears
lumbering through.
They may look big and scary
but they're afraid of you.

3 abolitionists
condemn slavery,
though standing up for what is right
took great bravery.

In the fight for freedom, scores of abolitionists—people who opposed slavery—spent time in Massachusetts where people of all backgrounds were sympathetic to their cause.

Sojourner Truth was born a slave. After being sold, she ran away and her freedom was bought by Quakers. As a free woman, she purchased property in Massachusetts where she became an outspoken advocate for both slaves and women.

Frederick Douglass escaped from slavery after teaching himself to read and write. He began speaking publicly in Massachusetts about his life, moving people to join the fight against slavery.

William Lloyd Garrison felt that slavery was against the laws of God. He shared his strong opinions on slavery for nearly 30 years in his newspaper, *The Liberator*.

three

3

4 Nantucket baskets—
each one smaller than the last,
first made by men at sea
on a wooden lightship mast.

Off the southern coast of Nantucket lie shallow-water sandbars called shoals which are a great danger to unsuspecting ships. One hundred and fifty years ago, ships with bright flashing lights were stationed in the water where it was impossible to build standing structures.

The men working on these lightships for long months would make baskets using the materials local whalers brought back from their travels and the techniques they had learned from Native Americans. They wove cane around the lightship masts, giving them a distinctive shape, and made them sturdy with wooden bases. The baskets became known as Nantucket lightship baskets.

In 1945 Philippino basket artist Jose Reyes moved to Nantucket and set up shop making covered baskets. The Reyes-style baskets, sometimes sold as purses, are usually decorated with ornamental scrimshaw, whalebone, or seashells, and are still popular today.

four

4

5 basketball players
dribble down the court.
A simple peach basket
started this sport.

Basketball was invented by Dr. James Naismith in Springfield, Massachusetts where he worked as a teacher. The challenge was to find a game that could be played indoors during the cold winters of New England. With a soccer ball and two peach baskets nailed to the balcony, Dr. Naismith taught 13 rules to his two teams, and basketball was born.

Today basketball is one of America's favorite sports. The Basketball Hall of Fame, a round building—shaped like a basketball—with twinkling lights, stands in Springfield not far from the site of that first game. Some of the most popular basketball players of all times have worn the green and white Boston Celtics uniform including Bill Russell and Larry Bird.

five

5

Crane Paper, which has been supplying the United States government with paper to make money since 1879, is located in Dalton, Massachusetts.

Anyone who has found a dollar bill in the pocket of a newly washed and dried pair of jeans knows money is more durable than regular paper. This is because of the special paper it is printed on—made of cotton and linen fibers with embedded silk threads. Even so, a one dollar bill only lasts about 18 months in circulation. So more than four billion are printed on Crane Paper each year. Other countries also use Crane Paper for their currency.

Some of the fabric Crane uses is recycled from clothing factories—even the denim that makes blue jeans. Besides money, Crane makes paper for other products as well, such as beautiful stationery and cards. Crane also produces other materials, some of which are used in cars and satellites.

six

6

6 dollar bills
to bring to the store.
When those are spent
Crane will make more.

The Black-capped Chickadee is the Massachusetts state bird. It is a small, very active white and black bird common throughout the state. A frequent visitor to backyard birdfeeders, the chickadee's call—"chick-a-dee dee dee"— can be heard in residential areas as well as in the forest. Chickadees eat mostly insects, seeds, and berries, depending on the season.

The female builds a nest out of moss and anything else soft she can find usually inside a hole in a tree. There she lays one egg every day for six to eight days. Both the mom and dad protect their pink-speckled eggs until the chicks hatch approximately 13 days later.

seven

7

7 chickadees
flitting around,
gathering seeds that have
fallen to the ground.

8 construction vehicles—
bulldozers and backhoes—
all to solve the city's
unending traffic woes.

Boston is a city with big traffic problems. In fact, for about 10 hours each day, cars driving on the main road through down-town, are bumper-to-bumper, sometimes not moving at all. In the 1950s when the Central Artery was built, more than 20,000 people had to move from their homes to make way for the construction. It was not a success. In fact, officials stopped construction of the road and made a tunnel. But this only made things worse.

Finally, to fix this problem, the Mass-achusetts Turnpike Authority made a plan to build a multi-lane underground expressway. The Big Dig, as it became known, began in 1991. Many sections have been opened. But there have also been problems along the way, including leaks in the tunnel walls under the har-bor, and parts of the ceilings falling in. Despite the cost and time, the end result should make driving easier and create a prettier downtown.

eight

8

Baseball is considered America's national pastime. But the Boston Red Sox have had the reputation of being baseball's heartbreak team for years because they had not won the World Series since 1918. A curse had long been blamed for their losing streak. This curse, it was said, had struck down all hopes of a series win since Babe Ruth—the game's most famous player—was sold by the Red Sox to the New York Yankees. Ruth then led the Yankees to numerous wins and titles, while the Red Sox began their years of heartbreak for fans and players alike.

But in 2004, the Red Sox came from behind to beat their archrival the Yankees in Game 7 for the American League Pennant. In the following World Series—the 100th—fans rejoiced as the curse was broken in four games, when the Red Sox beat the St. Louis Cardinals and became the World Champions.

nine

9

9 Red Sox
in four games straight,
break the longtime curse
of a baseball great.

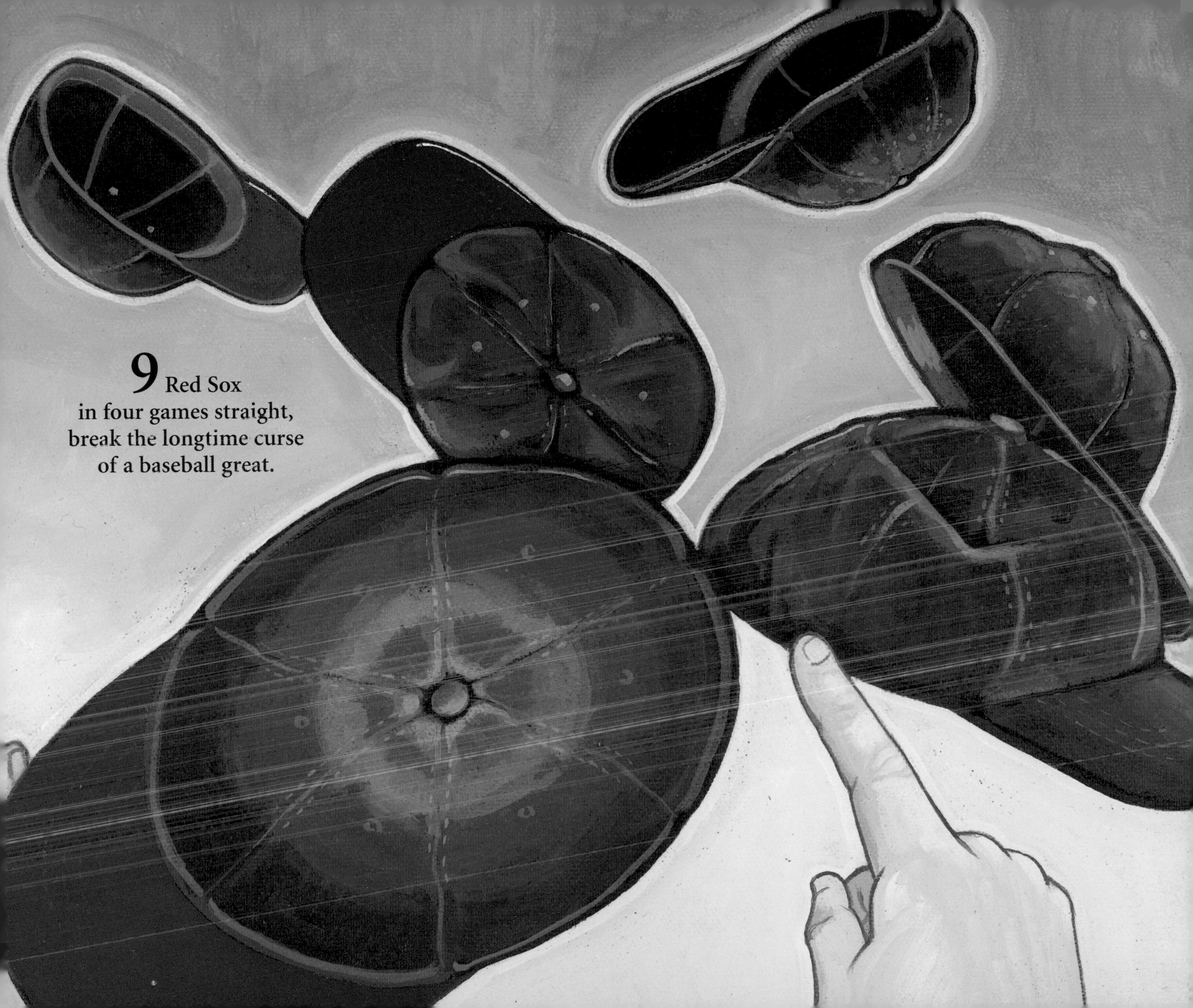

10 Yankee candles
scented spicy, warm, and sweet.
Some smell so delicious,
they seem good enough to eat.

In 1969 16-year-old Mike Kittredge of South Hadley, Massachusetts, made his first candle from melted crayons as a Christmas gift for his mother. A neighbor liked it so much, he sold her that candle and bought the ingredients to make two more. From there, Yankee Candle grew into a huge business. With stores in 42 states and more than 4,500 employees, Yankee Candle calls the small western Massachusetts town of South Deerfield home. There, at the flagship store, customers can purchase candles in such delicious sounding flavors as chocolate chip cookie, raspberry cream, and key lime pie. Visitors can also visit the Bavarian Christmas Village, the sweets shop, or even Santa's workshop. Kids can dip their own candles in colorful wax, and orders can be placed for customized party favors. The candles still come in colors reminiscent of the crayons that started it all. But now, drivers on Routes 5 and 10 can smell the sweet scent of candles in the air long before they see the long red barn that is Yankee Candle Company.

ten

10

11 wild turkeys,
stuffed and roasted,
at the first Thanksgiving
the Pilgrims hosted.

What we consider the first Thanksgiving was the feast after the Pilgrims' successful fall harvest in the year 1621. From firsthand accounts we know that a three-day feast was hosted by the Pilgrims. Like today, turkey was served, but along with it would have been duck, goose, and even swan.

The Wampanoag people, who had lived for many generations in the area the Pilgrims had settled into, kept the Pilgrims safe and taught them to raise corn. Massasoit, the Wampanoag leader, and his people were invited to share in the feast and 90 attended, bringing with them deer to add to the meal.

This festival giving thanks for the harvest was not, however, the beginning of an annual day of celebration. It was later, in 1863, that President Lincoln established the holiday in November to honor that first Thanksgiving feast.

By 1910 wild turkeys were close to extinction. But, today, thanks to biologists, they are common again in Massachusetts.

eleven

11

12 prehistoric footprints
left by dinos on the go,
trudging through the valley
200 million years ago.

The official Massachusetts state fossil is dinosaur tracks. The Connecticut River Valley that cuts through the western part of the state is rich with tracks from many different types of dinosaurs dating from about 200 million years ago. The first tracks were found in 1802 by a 17-year-old boy named Pliny Moody as he plowed his father's fields. At the time, scientists didn't even know what dinosaurs were, and these prints were thought to be from large ancient birds. Soon after Pliny's discovery, rocks being taken from quarries to pave streets contained what people thought were "turkey tracks." Edward Hitchcock, who later became the president of Amherst College, was called in to look at them. He began collecting, studying, and cataloging these finds in great detail. Today, his work is still used as scientific reference and his dinosaur footprint collection, now housed in the Amherst College Museum of Natural History, is the largest in the world.

twelve

12

Harriet Hanson earned $1.00 a week for work in the Lowell Mills in 1836 under poor conditions. When the mill's management planned to raise boarding-house fees, Harriet and 1,500 other girls decided to "turn out" or go on strike shutting the mills down. Though the strike did not win the girls what was needed in the end, it did give them a voice.

Other famous strikes in Massachusetts include the Lynn Shoemakers' strike of 1860, which began when the introduction of sewing machines cut jobs and wages. Strikebreakers were sent in, causing violent reactions from the workers. The Bread and Roses Strike of 1912 at the Lawrence textile mills ended when, under government pressure, the mill owners gave in. Eventually, though, the mills moved south where labor was cheaper. The Police Strike of 1919 set off rioting in Boston for three straight days. And in 2004, presidential candidate John Kerry refused to cross a Boston Police picket line to speak at the U.S. Conference of Mayors.

20 loud protesters
carry picket signs.
They ask for better wages
and that no one cross their lines.

HIGHER WAGES!
BETTER WAGES
WAGES!

30 athletes run
a twenty-six mile race
with thousands chasing after
at a marathon's pace.

On Patriot's Day every year since 1897, runners take to the streets of Boston and run the 26 miles and 385 yards of the Boston Marathon. It its first year, only 15 runners competed and the winner, John McDermott, finished in 2 hours, 55 minutes, and 10 seconds. On the Marathon's 100th anniversary in 1997, more than 37,000 people ran. The shortest recorded time for a runner to finish the Boston Marathon as of 2005, is two hours, seven minutes, and 15 seconds, by Cosmas Ndeti of Kenya in 1994.

Women didn't compete in the Boston Marathon until 1966 when Roberta Gibb ran unofficially. Six years later women were allowed to run and compete side by side with the men. A wheelchair division was added in 1975.

thirty

30

A specialty of Massachusetts is the white, creamy variety of clam chowder called Boston or New England clam chowder. In most recipes ingredients include milk or cream, potatoes, and, of course, clams.

The clam is a bivalve—meaning it has a shell made up of two halves—and comes in soft or hard shells. The largest of the hard-shelled clams, often used in chowder, is the quahog. The smaller quahogs are called cherrystones or littlenecks. Fresh clams should be tightly closed and will open when cooked. It takes about 40 fresh clams to make a big pot of Boston clam chowder, but many cooks simply use canned clams.

forty

40

40 quahog clams
to cook up just right—
hot chowder tastes delicious
on a chilly Boston night.

M is for Mayflower
2

50 children's books
on the library shelf
to read with Mom and Dad
or all by yourself.

Boston, Massachusetts is the site of American's first free lending library and the first with a children's room.

Theodor Seuss Geisel, better known as Dr. Suess, was born in Springfield, Massachusetts. *The Cat In The Hat* was his most famous book, but his first book *And To Think That I Saw It On Mulberry Street* was rejected 27 times before it was published.

Many authors and illustrators of children's books live or have lived in Massachusetts. Eric Carle and his Museum of Children's Book Art are here as well as Caldecott winners Robert McCloskey, Mordicai Gerstein, Barbara Cooney, Norton Juster and Newberry winners Patricia MacLachlan and Lois Lowry. Also making their home in Massachusetts are author Jane Yolen and illustrator Jan Brett who are both related to this book—can you guess how?

fifty

50

Massachusetts has many miles of coastline, some of it treacherous. To keep sailors safe, especially before the invention of computer navigation, more than 60 lighthouses were built. Many of these no longer exist, but 49 still stand.

The lighthouse on Race Point, Cape Cod, was erected in 1816. Its revolving light, 25 feet above sea level, was one of the first of its kind. Until the 1930s when a beach vehicle was made for them, the lighthouse keeper's children walked three miles each day to go to school. After 1972 when the lighthouse was automated and keepers were no longer needed, no more families lived there. Today, the Race Point Lighthouse's light still helps keep sailors safe, and tourists can rent an overnight room in the keeper's house.

60 lighthouses
once signaled sailors' way
for safe passage at night
or on a foggy day.

70 snowflakes
just beginning to fall
will become a nor'easter's
wintry squall.

Though Massachusetts weather ranges from muggy and almost unbearably hot in the summer to bitter cold in the winter, what the state is most known for is its blizzards. A nor'easter is a storm that churns just off the coast from the northeast. This type of storm's warm air turns to precipitation over land. When things turn cold, this creates lots of snow.

Some years, Massachusetts has almost no snow. But sometimes the state gets so much that schools are cancelled and the highways are shut down until plows and sand and salt trucks can make the roads safe.

Memorable snowstorms that have blanketed Massachusetts in white include the blizzard of 1888 which surprised the state in March, killing 400 people and sinking 200 ships. More recently, the blizzard of 1978 dropped 55 inches of snow on the state, leaving many people without power or any way to leave their homes.

seventy

70

Conversation Hearts, the sugary candies with cute sayings on them, are made by the New England Confectionery Company, or Necco, in Cambridge, Massachusetts.

In 1847, Oliver R. Chase invented and patented the first American candy machine. Soon after, he invented a machine for pulverizing sugar. These inventions, combined with the use of steam power, made factory production of candy much faster. Oliver and his brother Silas founded a candy company which eventually became Necco.

During World War II, like many U.S. factories, Necco handed over control of part of its factory to make war materials. But, ever since 1866, Necco has been making the heart candies, originally called Motto Hearts. Eight billion hearts are made and sold between January 1 and February 14 every year just in time for Valentine's Day.

eighty

80

80 candy hearts
for your valentine,
each one asking sweetly
will you please "Be mine?"

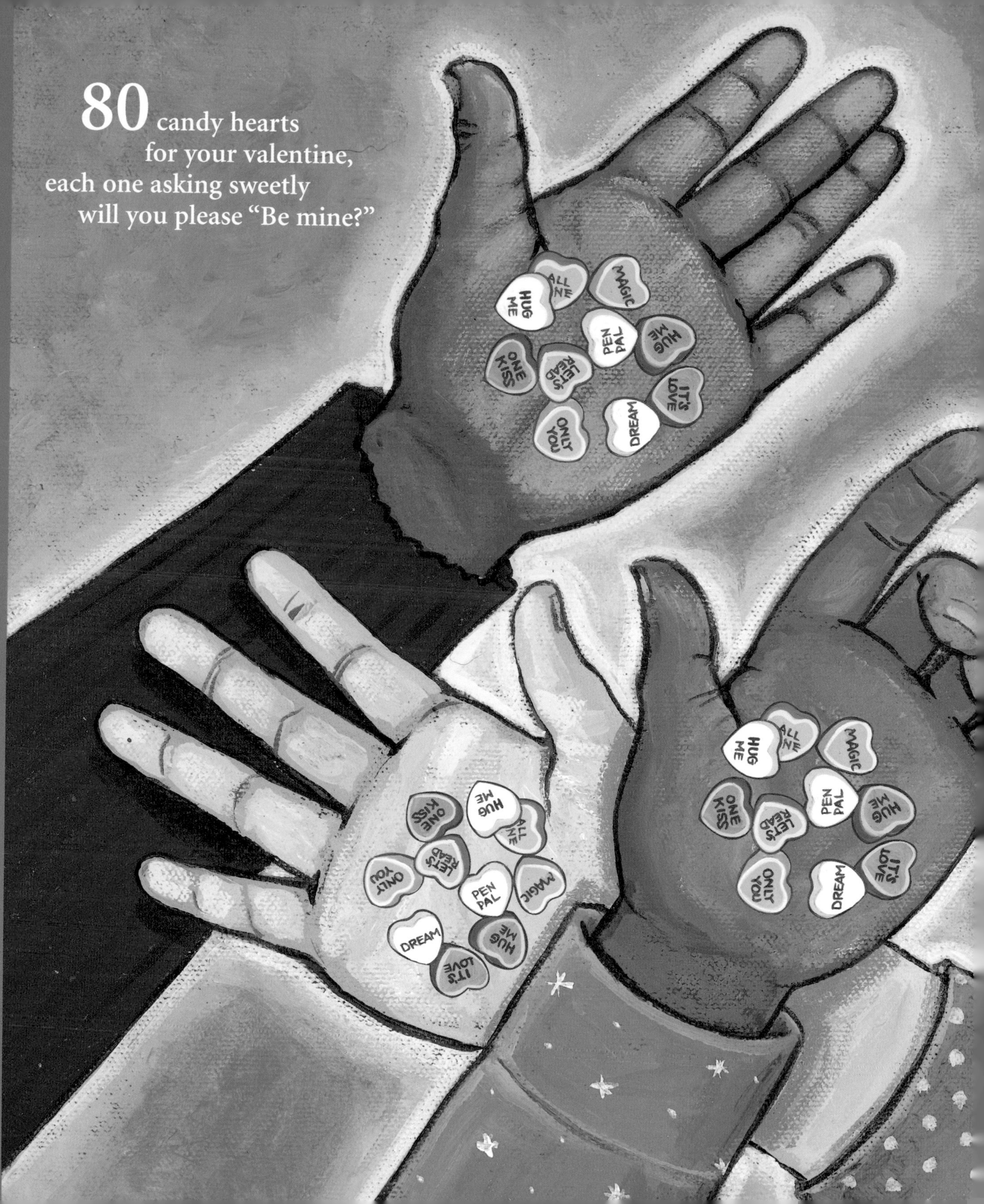

MAGIC
HUG ME
PEN PAL
IT'S LOVE
HUG ME
LET'S READ
DREAM
ONE KISS
ONLY YOU

Johnny Appleseed is the official Massachusetts state folk hero. He was born John Chapman in Leominster in 1774 as the town was preparing for war against England. His love of the outdoors grew in Longmeadow, a rural town in the southwestern part of the state—apple orchard country—where John was raised. As a young man, he set out on his own toward the west, where the legend of Johnny Appleseed began.

The truth, or at least as close as historians can tell, is that John Chapman sold apple seeds and seedlings and cultivated orchards across the country. A gentle, well-spoken man, he also preached Christian values and acted as a go-between with settlers and Native Americans. He bought land in Indiana and planted 15,000 apple trees. One hundred and fifty years later, apples still grow on some of John Chapman's trees and every student in the United States learns the very American legend of Johnny Appleseed.

ninety

90

90 apple seeds
lovingly sewn.
John Chapman's legacy—
orchards full grown.

100 red bricks
on a walk through history
teaching everyone about
our journey to be free.

The State House

The Robert Gould Regiment Memorial

King's Chapel

Old South Meeting House

Old State House

The Boston Common

Massachusetts was one of the early areas colonized by Europeans in the New World. Many American firsts occurred here.

In Boston, the state capital, there is a 2.5 mile walking tour marked with red bricks and paint called the Freedom Trail. Included in the 16 historical stops is America's first public school where patriots Samuel Adams, John Hancock, and Benjamin Franklin were educated. You can visit the Old South Meeting House where colonists gathered to protest Britain's tea taxes just before the Boston Tea Party. Along the way is the Old State House where the Declaration of Independence was read aloud for the first time. Other stops include Old Ironsides, the Boston Commons, and the Old North Church were Paul Revere watched for a sign–lights to be hung warning of the British troops' arrival: one if by land, two if by sea.

one hundred

100

Heidi E.Y. Stemple

Heidi Elisabet Yolen Stemple grew up in Hatfield, Massachusetts, and after 18 years of living elsewhere, she has returned. She has also returned to the family business—writing children's books—after working as a probation/parole officer, a private investigator, and a bartender. Her mother, with whom she has worked for 12 years on books including *Dear Mother, Dear Daughter* and *The Barefoot Book of Ballet Stories*, is author Jane Yolen. Heidi has two daughters, Maddison and Glendon.

Though Heidi did not want to be a writer like her mom when she was growing up, now she cannot imagine doing anything else. Her two favorite kinds of books to write are rhyming books and nonfiction, so this book was perfect for her.

Jeannie Brett

Jeannie Brett enjoys visiting elementary schools around New England, sharing her original artwork, her love of the natural world, and her excitement of illustrating children's books. Jeannie studied at the School of the Museum of Fine Arts in Boston and at the Minneapolis College of Art and Design. She lives in York, Maine, with her husband Greg, and their three children, Gregory, Sophie, and Lee. They share their home with a horse named Bailey, a wonderful Newfoundland dog, Cali, and two enormous cats (brothers) Macaroni and Tortellini. In additional to a lengthy list of independent, illustrative work, *One if by Land* is her fourth children's book published by Sleeping Bear Press. She also illustrated the companion title, *M is for Mayflower: A Massachusetts Alphabet.*